Happy Birthday,
Penelope   2018

For my dear friends—

Bud and Esther,
Don and Helen,
Emery,
Ceil,
Hazel,
and Joan.

Also in memory of Carl.

Follow and Do
The Apostles' Creed

Written and Illustrated by Joni Walker

CONCORDIA PUBLISHING HOUSE • SAINT LOUIS

Dear Parents,

Webster's defines "creed" as "a brief authoritative formula of religious belief; a set of fundamental beliefs; a guiding principle." We confess the Apostles' Creed, as well as the two other creeds of the Christian church, as a statement of our faith in the Triune God. The Apostles' Creed is also known as the baptismal creed. It is confessed by the church at Baptism because we are baptized at Christ's command in the name of the Triune God.

The Creed is a concise, emphatic summary of what Scripture teaches about God the Father, Son, and Holy Spirit. Since the second or third century, Christians across the ages and around the world have spoken these words to express what we believe God does in our world and in our lives.

After they teach their children the Lord's Prayer, many parents teach the Apostles' Creed so their young ones can continue to learn about worshiping God and learn how to receive God's gifts in the church service. Regardless when parents choose to teach about the faith, when they do, they are fulfilling their calling as Christian parents. "Let the word of Christ dwell in you richly as you teach and admonish one another with all wisdom, and as you SING psalms, hymns and spiritual songs with gratitude in your hearts to God" (Colossians 3:16).

Young children learn through all their senses. They remember experiences and they like repetition. Because they delight in memorizing, children readily learn to say the Creed and absorb the meaning of its three articles: that God the Father created us, God the Son redeemed us, and God the Holy Spirit sanctifies us.

The tone and cadence of the Creed spoken in church becomes a lasting MEMORY that is combined with other sensory dynamics, such as music, sights, smells, and the like. And when our children hear us say these words in church week after week, they begin to understand and appreciate our faith in God as well. As they do, they see themselves—and us—as God's baptized, forgiven, and redeemed children.

I believe in God, the Father Almighty,
Maker of heaven and earth.

God created
the world.

5

WHAT DOES THIS MEAN?

I believe that God has made me and all creatures; that He has given me my body and soul, eyes, ears, and all my members, my reason and all my senses, and still takes care of them.

God made each of us special.

He also gives me clothing and shoes, food and drink, house and home, wife and children, land, animals, and all I have. He richly and daily provides me with all that I need to support this body and life.

I am thankful for
the family
God gave me.

He defends me against all danger and guards
and protects me from all evil. All this He does only out
of fatherly, divine goodness and mercy, without any
merit or worthiness in me. For all this it is my duty
to thank and praise, serve and obey Him.
This is most certainly true.

Thank You
God,
for protecting
me.

11

The Second Article–Redemption

And in Jesus Christ, His only Son, our Lord, who was conceived by the Holy Spirit, born of the Virgin Mary, suffered under Pontius Pilate, was crucified, died and was buried. He descended into hell. The third day He rose again from the dead. He ascended into heaven and sits at the right hand of God, the Father Almighty. From thence He will come to judge the living and the dead.

I am glad Jesus died to take my sins away.

13

WHAT DOES THIS MEAN?

I believe that Jesus Christ true God, begotten of the Father from eternity, and also true man, born of the Virgin Mary, is my Lord, who has redeemed me, a lost and condemned person, purchased and won me from all sins, from death, and from the power of the devil; not with gold or silver, but with His holy, precious blood and with His innocent suffering and death, that I may be His own and live under Him in His kingdom and serve Him in everlasting righteousness, innocence, and blessedness, just as He is risen from the dead, lives and reigns to all eternity. This is most certainly true.

The Third Article–Sanctification

I believe in the Holy Spirit, the holy
Christian church, the communion of saints,
the forgiveness of sins, the resurrection of
the body, and the life everlasting. Amen.

I love to be with my family in church.

17

WHAT DOES THIS MEAN?

I believe that I cannot by my own reason or strength believe in Jesus Christ, my Lord, or come to Him; but the Holy Spirit has called me by the Gospel, enlightened me with His gifts, sanctified and kept me in the true faith.

In the same way He calls, gathers, enlightens, and sanctifies the whole Christian church on earth, and keeps it with Jesus Christ in the one true faith. In this Christian church He daily and richly forgives all my sins and the sins of all believers.

20

On the Last Day He will raise me and all the dead, and give eternal life to me and all believers in Christ. This is most certainly true.

22

I will see great-grandpa
and grandma in heaven Someday.

Published by Concordia Publishing House
3558 S. Jefferson Avenue, St. Louis, MO 63118-3968
1-800-325-3040 • www.cph.org

Manufactured in China

1   2   3   4   5   6   7   8   9   10   14 13 12 11 10 09 08 07 06 05